PS 157
757 CAULDWELL AVENUE
BRONX, NY 10456

3GRHI000040559

The Bald Eagle
Yanuck, Debbie L.

RL: 3.6 IL: K-3

Fountas & Pinnell: N

First Facts

American Symbols

The Bald Eagle

W9-CIL-798

by Debbie L. Yanuck

Consultant:
Melodie Andrews, Ph.D.
Associate Professor of Early American History
Minnesota State University, Mankato

Capstone
press

Capstone Press
1710 Roe Crest Drive, North Mankato, Minnesota 56003
www.capstonepub.com

Copyright © 2003 by Capstone Press, a Capstone imprint. All rights reserved.
No part of this publication may be reproduced in whole or in part, or stored in a retrieval
system, or transmitted in any form or by any means, electronic, mechanical, photocopying,
recording, or otherwise, without written permission of the publisher.
For information regarding permission, write to Capstone Press,
1710 Roe Crest Drive, North Mankato, Minnesota 56003.
Printed in the United States of America in North Mankato, Minnesota.

072014
008336R

Library of Congress Cataloging-in-Publication Data
Yanuck, Debbie L.
    The bald eagle / by Debbie L. Yanuck.
    p. cm.—(American symbols)
    Summary: Information on bald eagles accompanies an introduction to how this bird
became a symbol of the United States.
    Includes bibliographical references and index.
    ISBN-13: 978-0-7368-1629-8 (hardcover)   ISBN-10: 0-7368-1629-1 (hardcover)
    ISBN-13: 978-0-7368-4700-1 (softcover pbk.)   ISBN-10: 0-7368-4700-6 (softcover pbk.)
    1. United States—Seal—Juvenile literature. 2. Bald Eagle—Juvenile literature.
3. Emblems, National—United States—Juvenile literature. 4. Animals—Symbolic aspects—
Juvenile literature. [1. United States—Seal. 2. Bald Eagle. 3. Eagles. 4. Emblems, National.
5. Signs and symbols.] I. Title. II. American symbols (Mankato, Minn.)
CD5610 .Y36 2003
929.9'0973—dc21   2002010712

Editorial Credits
Chris Harbo and Roberta Schmidt, editors; Eric Kudalis, product planning editor;
    Linda Clavel, cover and interior designer; Alta Schaffer, photo researcher

Photo Credits
Corbis/Walter Hodges, 19 (left)
Hulton Archive by Getty Images, 10, 13 (left)
Library of Congress, 13 (right)
PhotoDisc, cover (right)
Stock Montage, Inc., cover (left), 15
Tom & Pat Leeson, 5, 7, 9, 11, 16, 17, 21
U.S. Treasury, 19 (right), 20

Table of Contents

Bald Eagle Fast Facts

- Bald eagles only live in North America.

- Benjamin Franklin wanted the wild turkey to be the national bird.

- In 1782, Congress made the bald eagle the national bird.

- The bald eagle is on the Great Seal. The Great Seal was created in 1782.

- The Great Seal often is stamped on important papers signed by the President.

- A pesticide called DDT almost caused the bald eagle to die out completely.

- Today, most of the 70,000 bald eagles live in Alaska, Florida, and Canada.

Freedom, Strength, and Courage

The bald eagle is an American symbol of freedom, strength, and courage. In the late 1700s, the American colonists fought for independence from Great Britain. The bald eagle is a symbol of the colonists' courage to fight.

independence
freedom from the control of other people or things

North America's Bird

Map legend:
- Summer
- All Year
- Winter
- Country Boundary

Alaska (U.S.)

PACIFIC OCEAN

CANADA

UNITED STATES

ATLANTIC OCEAN

MEXICO

GULF OF MEXICO

Bald Eagle Range

Bald eagles live only in North America. Some adult bald eagles stand 3 feet (0.9 meters) tall. An adult eagle's wingspan can be 7 feet

(2.1 meters). Bald eagles can live up to 30 years in the wild. They are not bald. Bald eagles have white feathers on their heads.

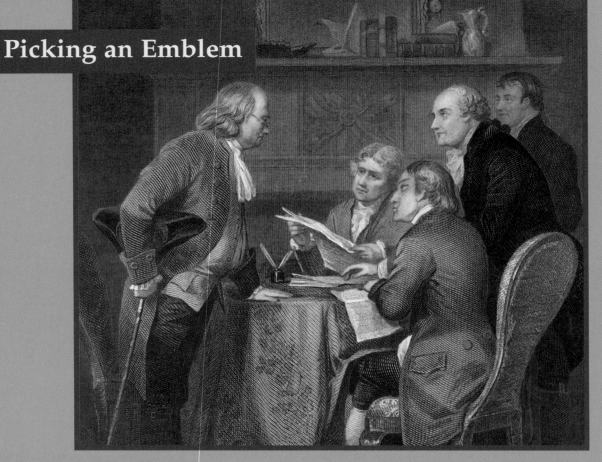

In 1776, Congress wanted an emblem to represent the United States. John Adams, Benjamin Franklin, and Thomas Jefferson were picked to create the emblem.

Franklin wanted the wild turkey on the emblem. Like the bald eagle, the wild turkey lives only in North America. Others did not want the turkey on the emblem.

National Symbol

By 1782, the United States still needed an emblem. Charles Thomson saw a drawing of a bald eagle. He made some changes to the drawing. In June 1782, Congress put Thomson's design on the Great Seal. The bald eagle became a national symbol.

Charles Thomson

James Trenchard's engraving of
Charles Thomson's drawing

The Great Seal

The Great Seal shows a bald eagle with a shield on its chest. The shield has 13 stripes. The stripes stand for America's first 13 colonies. The eagle holds an olive branch and 13 arrows. The olive branch stands for peace. The arrows stand for war.

shield
a piece of armor used to protect the body from attack

Bald Eagles in Danger

In the mid-1900s, bald eagles nearly died out. A pesticide called DDT had poisoned rivers and fish. Bald eagles ate the fish. Eagle eggshells then became too thin.

Many eaglets died before they could hatch.
In 1972, the U.S. government banned DDT.
Today, more than 70,000 bald eagles live in
North America.

pesticide
a chemical used to kill insects
and other pests that eat crops

The Symbol Today

The bald eagle remains an important symbol. The U.S. Postal Service uses a picture of the bald eagle in its logo. The Great Seal is printed on the back of the U.S. one dollar bill. The bald eagle reminds people of freedom, strength, and courage.

logo
a symbol that represents a group
or company

Timeline

1776—John Adams, Benjamin Franklin, and Thomas Jefferson are asked to design an emblem for the United States.

1940—Congress passes a law making it illegal to catch or kill bald eagles.

1782—Charles Thomson's design of the bald eagle is chosen as the emblem of the United States.

1972—The United States government bans the use of the pesticide DDT.

1970—Scientists estimate that there are less than 1,000 bald eagles left in the United States.

Present—More than 70,000 bald eagles live throughout North America.

Hands On: Make an Emblem

The Great Seal represents the United States. It often is stamped on important papers signed by the President. The Great Seal shows the bald eagle as a symbol of America's courage, strength, and freedom. What kinds of things represent you? Make an emblem that is a symbol of you.

What You Need

Clay   Ink pad
Pencil   White paper

What You Do

1. Roll a piece of clay into a ball. The ball should be the size of a baseball.
2. Flatten the ball to a thickness of about an inch (2.5 centimeters).
3. Think about activities you like to do or sports you like to play.
4. Use a pencil to carve a picture of your favorite activity into the clay. Make the grooves deep. The picture will be your emblem.
5. Let the clay dry overnight.
6. When the clay is dry, press your emblem into the ink pad. Then press your emblem on a piece of paper. Now you have your own seal that is a symbol of you.

Words to Know

ban (BAN)—to forbid something

colony (KOL-uh-nee)—an area that has been settled by people from another country; a colony is ruled by another country.

Congress (KONG-griss)—the branch of the U.S. government that makes laws

eaglet (EE-glit)—a young eagle

emblem (EM-bluhm)—a symbol or a sign that stands for something

freedom (FREE-duhm)—the right to live the way you want

pesticide (PESS-tuh-side)—a chemical used to kill insects and other pests that eat crops

symbol (SIM-buhl)—an object that stands for something else

Read More

Binns, Tristan Boyer. *The Bald Eagle.* Symbols of Freedom. Chicago: Heinemann Library, 2001.

Wilson, Jon. *The American Eagle: The Symbol of America.* Chanhassen, Minn.: Child's World, 1999.

Internet Sites

Track down many sites about the bald eagle.

Visit the FACT HOUND at
http://www.facthound.com

IT IS EASY! IT IS FUN!

1) Go to *http://www.facthound.com*
2) Type in: 0736816291
3) Click on "FETCH IT" and FACT HOUND will find several links hand-picked by our editors.

Relax and let our pal FACT HOUND do the research for you!

Index